Practise Your Spelling Skills

THIRD EDITION

2

John Rose

Pearson Australia
(a division of Pearson Australia Group)
707 Collins Street, Melbourne, Victoria 3008
PO Box 23360, Melbourne, Victoria 8012
www.pearson.com.au

Copyright © Pearson Australia 2006
(a division of Pearson Australia Group Pty Ltd)

First published 2006 by Pearson Australia
Reprinted 2007, 2008, 2010, 2011 (twice), 2013, 2014

Edited by Anne McKenna
Cover and interior design by Kim Ferguson
Illustrations by Christina Miesen
Cover image by Getty Images
Prepress work by The Type Factory
Produced by Pearson Australia
Printed in Malaysia (CTP-VVP)

ISBN 978-0-7339-7818-0

Contents

To the teacher

Spelling and writing

This spelling program has been prepared in response to a defined need. Spelling is one of the sub-skills of writing along with appropriate syntactical structures, punctuation, vocabulary development and handwriting. Writing activities in the primary school should, wherever possible, emphasise the interrelatedness of these sub-skills as well as of the other areas of language—listening, speaking and reading.

Spelling ability grows most effectively when spelling is viewed as an integral part of the total language programs, and is developed through a continuous program that recognises both increasing ability and changing interests of the writer. As children develop the desire to communicate their ideas in writing, they need skills in spelling that can be provided systematically. The skills and the appropriate experiences can, in many instances, go hand in hand.

In this book ...

This book contains forty units, four of which are revision units.

Twenty-nine units are based on common elements found in words often used by children at this age such as **ea** and **ck**. Two units contain essential (frequently used) words and a further five units are theme-based.

Activities are varied and are based around the word lists. Overall, the book is sequential in nature and provides a comprehensive cover of the spelling requirements for children at this stage.

Challenge words are also included in some of the units to further extend fast-finishers. All of the list words are provided at the end of the book. Space for children to compile their own lists of words is provided on pages 86 to 91, as it is recognised that teachers will be using additional thematic words, according to what is of current interest in the classroom, to supplement the list words in this book.

Features of this book

Common letter pattern

Word list with common letter pattern highlighted

Word list for Theme unit (five in book)

Word list for Essential words unit (two in book)

Revision unit (four in book)

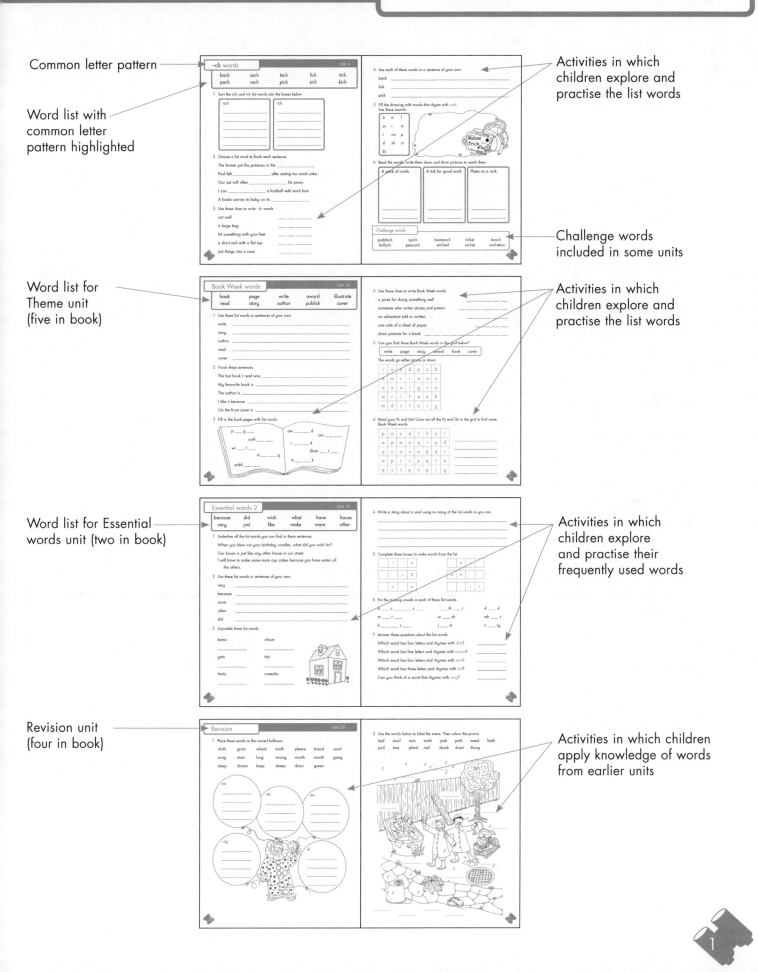

Activities in which children explore and practise the list words

Challenge words included in some units

Activities in which children explore and practise the list words

Activities in which children explore and practise their frequently used words

Activities in which children apply knowledge of words from earlier units

ar words

card	hard	bar	shark	smart
yard	far	star	part	start

1 Write two list words that rhyme with each of the words below.

yard _____ _____

bar _____ _____

part _____ _____

2 Use one of the list words to finish each of these sentences.

The toffee was too _____ for me to eat.

The _____ swam in the sea.

We saw the _____ in the sky.

My friend gave me a birthday _____.

Do you live very _____ from the school?

3 Draw a picture to match each of these words.

star	shark	card

4 Use these clues to write **ar** words.

a long way ___ ___ ___   clever ___ ___ ___ ___ ___

not soft ___ ___ ___ ___   a piece ___ ___ ___ ___

begin something ___ ___ ___ ___ ___

5 Put the **ar**, **ard** and **art** list words in the correct boxes.

ar	ard	art
_____	_____	_____
_____	_____	_____
	_____	_____

6 Unjumble these **ar** words.

arshk   mtsar   arhd

_____   _____   _____

tarp   arb   astr

_____   _____   _____

7 Use these words in sentences of your own.

card _____

hard _____

bar _____

part _____

start _____

8 Finish the **ar** words in the shark.

y ____ ____ d   sh ____ ____ k

sm ____ ____ t

st ____ ____

c ____ ____ d

sh– words

shed	shot	shop	shy	shock
ship	shut	shin	shell	short

1 Choose a list word to finish each sentence.

My father is tall, but I am _____.

I like to buy lollies at the _____.

'Please _____ the door,' said the teacher.

My bike is in our _____.

A _____ is a very large boat.

2 Use these clues to write sh– words.

afraid to meet people ___ ___ ___

a small hut ___ ___ ___ ___

not long ___ ___ ___ ___ ___

the thin covering around an egg ___ ___ ___ ___ ___

a part of the leg ___ ___ ___ ___

3 Unjumble these sh– words.

elshl   kcosh   ishn

_____   _____   _____

4 Draw circles around the little words you can find in the bigger words.

Find hut in shut.   Find hop in shop.

Find in in shin.   Find hip in ship.

5 Draw four things from the list. Write their names.

_____ _____ _____ _____

6 Add the letter **s** to make these words plural.

shed _____   ship _____   shell _____   shop _____

7 Circle the **sh–** words in the columns below.

shed	shock	south	shell	sound
sharp	mouth	ship	whale	count
spent	shy	shin	chin	stunt
shot	shut	shop	short	sweet

8 Read the words, write them down and draw pictures to match them.

A tin shed	A pink shell	A short man

_____ _____ _____

_____ _____ _____

rash	rush	push	wash	bush
brush	crush	fresh	blush	finish

1 Use list words to complete the following.

Three words that start with **b** _____ _____ _____

Any word with five letters _____ _____ _____

_____

The longest word in the list _____

2 Draw a green bush, a boy with a rash, and a fresh chocolate donut.

3 Which list words go with the other words?

tree   shrub   hedge   _____

end   stop   complete   _____

squash   squeeze   press   _____

hurry   run   speed   _____

4 Write these letters in alphabetical order.

r p w b _____

Now write these words in alphabetical order.

wash   brush   rash   push

_____

5 Write the list word that goes with each picture.

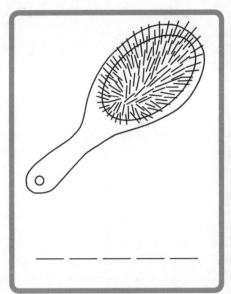
_ _ _ _ _

_ _ _ _ _

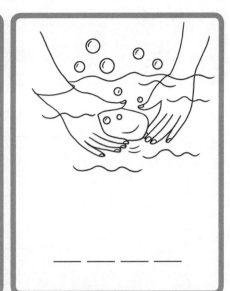
_ _ _ _ _

6 Add **ed** to the list word at the left to finish each sentence.

rush   I _____ my breakfast because I was running late.

brush   After breakfast I _____ my teeth.

push   I _____ open the gate and ran into my school yard.

blush   I _____ when I suddenly remembered it was

Saturday.

7 Use these clues to write list words.

a thick shrub   _____

something we use for sweeping   _____

to dash forward   _____

spots on the skin when you are ill   _____

Did you know?

A brush is also the name for a fox's tail and a rush is a water plant.

–ck words

back	sack	tack	lick	tick
pack	rack	pick	sick	kick

1 Sort the **ack** and **ick** list words into the boxes below.

ack

_____

_____

_____

_____

_____

ick

_____

_____

_____

_____

_____

2 Choose a list word to finish each sentence.

The farmer put the potatoes in the _____.

Paul felt _____ after eating too much cake.

Our cat will often _____ his paws.

I can _____ a football with each foot.

A koala carries its baby on its _____.

3 Use these clues to write –ck words.

not well   ___ ___ ___ ___

a large bag   ___ ___ ___ ___

hit something with your feet ___ ___ ___ ___

a short nail with a flat top ___ ___ ___ ___

put things into a case   ___ ___ ___ ___

8

4 Use each of these words in a sentence of your own.

back _____

lick _____

pick _____

5 Fill the drawing with words that rhyme with sack.
Use these sounds:

b	tr	l
sn	r	st
t	sm	p
sl	sh	cr
bl		

Mouse Trick
Game 2-4 players

6 Read the words, write them down and draw pictures to match them.

A pack of cards	A tick for good work	Plates on a rack
_____	_____	_____
_____	_____	_____

Challenge words

paddock	quick	hammock	ticket	knock
bullock	peacock	wicked	rocket	cockatoo

th– words

they	these	this	thick	thank
them	those	thin	think	three

1 Choose a list word to finish each sentence.

Sue has two pencils, but she cannot find _____.

An elephant has very _____ legs.

Sam brought _____ baby rabbits to school.

_____ were very small.

_____ is my best writing.

2 Unjumble these th– words.

cithk   kntha   reeth

_____   _____   _____

3 Can you find these th– words in the grid below?

The words go either across or down.

these
those
this
they
three
thin
them
thick

s	t	h	i	c	k	t
t	h	e	s	e	i	h
h	r	t	h	i	n	i
e	e	t	h	e	m	s
y	e	t	h	o	s	e

10

4 Circle the **th–** words in these columns.

these	those	sleep	tree	them	tent	this
they	stunt	plant	sheet	thin	there	chant
thick	blunt	smoke	think	thank	three	smart

5 Use these words in sentences of your own.

they _____

those _____

thank _____

this _____

three _____

6 Read the words, write them down and draw pictures to match them.

A thin person	Three red apples	A thick pencil
_____	_____	_____
_____	_____	_____

7 Underline any list words you can find in these sentences.

Those thick crayons belong to Claire.

I think she got them for her birthday.

Claire is six and her sister is three.

They live in this street near the school.

11

–nk words

bank	tank	spank	sink	drink
sank	thank	pink	wink	think

1 Sort the **ink** and **ank** words into the boxes below.

ink

_____

_____

_____

_____

ank

_____

_____

_____

_____

2 Use these words in sentences of your own.

wink _____

spank _____

thank _____

drink _____

think _____

3 What do these sentences tell you? The answers are words that rhyme with link.

Dirty dishes are washed in me. _____

I close one eye. _____

I am a colour. _____

4 Add the letter **s** to make these words plural.

bank ____   tank ____   drink ____   sink ____

5 Write **–nk** words in the fish. Use the grassy letters to help you.

pi   sa   ta   tha   dri   spa

6 Add **ing** to each of these words and then read the new words aloud.

drink ____ ____ ____   think ____ ____ ____   wink ____ ____ ____

Now use them in sentences of your own.

drinking _____

thinking _____

winking _____

7 Choose a list word to finish each sentence.

The ship _____ after it crashed onto the rocks.

I took my money to the _____.

Kim's favourite colour is _____.

I _____ green is a better colour.

The petrol was stored in a large _____.

Maths words

numbers	estimate	shapes	square	measure
subtraction	add	answers	circle	counting

1 My Year 2 maths book has these directions. Read them and underline any list words.

Use icy-pole sticks, paper clips and pencils to estimate and then measure the
   length of these objects.

Use the numbers in each box to write a number sentence.

Add the numbers on the dice and write the answers in the boxes.

Circle the shapes in the box to make groups of ten.

Finish this pattern, counting by 2s.

Answer the addition and subtraction facts by counting on.

2 Draw a square and a circle, and write your favourite number.

3 Write these letters in alphabetical order.

s   m   a   e   _____

Now write these words in alphabetical order.

measure   estimate   add   square

_____

4 Draw circles around the little words you can find in the bigger words.

Find mate in estimate.   Find ape in shapes.

Find are in square.   Find sure in measure.

Find act in subtraction.   Find tin in counting.

5 Unjumble these list words.

erccil   gnuocnti   wesnars

_____   _____   _____

6 Use list words to complete the following.

a word with three letters   _____

a word starting with **sh**   _____

the longest word   _____

a word starting with **e**   _____

two words starting with **c**   _____   _____

7 Use the given word to finish each sentence.

numbers   I can spell all the _____ from one to ten.

square   A _____ has four sides that are the same size.

measure   Our class had to _____ how much water was
                in the bucket.

estimate   First our group had to _____ the length of the
                book, then measure it.

8 Finish these list words.

subtract ___ ___ ___   answ ___ ___ s   ___ ___ apes

count ___ ___ ___   numb ___ ___ s   m ___ ___ sure

More maths words				
cone	sphere	even	width	area
cube	odd	length	triangle	multiply

–nt words

tent	lent	ant	chant	hint
went	bent	pant	mint	print

1 Write two list words that rhyme with each of the words below.

went _____   _____

ant _____   _____

hint _____   _____

2 Choose a list word to finish each sentence.

An _____ is a very small insect.

When we went camping, we slept in a _____.

Little Red Riding Hood _____ to visit her grandmother.

Carol tried to put the pin through the cardboard, but it _____.

My brother can _____ neatly.

3 Sort the **ant**, **ent** and **int** list words into the boxes.

ant	ent	int
_____	_____	_____
_____	_____	_____
_____	_____	_____
	_____	

4 Use these list words in sentences of your own.

print   _____

chant   _____

lent   _____

5 Read the words, write them down and draw pictures to match them.

A bent nail	An ant on a leaf	A tent in the rain
_____	_____	_____
_____	_____	_____

6 Add **ing** to each of these words, then read the new words aloud.

pant ____ ____ ____   chant ____ ____ ____   print ____ ____ ____

Now use them in sentences of your own.

panting   _____

chanting   _____

printing   _____

Challenge words

grunt	splint	mountain	dentist	discount
event	count	slant	splinter	glint

17

Essential words 1

about	after	all	are	back	our
came	could	friend	from	get	going

1 Choose a list word to finish each sentence.

I am so hungry I _____ eat three ice-creams.

Where _____ you going after the netball match?

The camel had a huge hump on its _____.

I made a new _____ at camp last summer.

2

b	s	g	o	u	f
a	b	o	u	t	r
c	g	i	r	f	i
k	e	n	a	r	e
r	t	g	r	o	n
c	a	m	e	m	d

Can you find nine of the list words hidden in the grid? Write them down.

_____ _____

_____ _____

_____ _____

_____ _____

_____

3 Put a circle around each correct word in the brackets.

I always clean my teeth (all, after) breakfast.

The parcel came (from, about) my uncle.

It rained (all, from) last night and the thunder kept me awake.

My pa (could, friend) ride a bucking horse when he was young.

4 Unjumble these list words.

aemc _____   ggnoi _____   buoat _____

retfa _____   lcduo _____   lal _____

5 In the box below draw your friend. Write a sentence about your friend.

_____

_____

6 Write list words to complete the following.

the longest word   _____

words that have **ou** in them   _____ _____ _____

words that have four letters   _____ _____ _____

words that have a **t** in them   _____ _____ _____

7 Which list word can fit into both these sentences?

A snail carries a shell on its _____.

Mum said she was going shopping but would be _____ in about ten minutes.

Revision

1 Place these words in the correct balloons.

shed   tent   star   print   smart   start   finish

tack   rack   fresh   hint   chant   ship   bar

blush   sick   shock   kick   push   shell

–nt

_____
_____
_____

sh–

_____
_____
_____

–ck

_____
_____
_____

ar

_____
_____
_____

–sh

_____
_____
_____

2 In these boxes, finish the words and match them with pictures, or write words to match the drawings.

te __ __	__ __ __ __	sh __ __
__ __ __ __	sa __ __	__ __ __ __
ca __ __	__ __ __ __ __	a __ __
__ __ __ __	st __ __	__ __ __ __

21

–th words

moth	tooth	mouth	path	with
cloth	teeth	month	bath	both

1 Choose a list word to finish each sentence.

The first _____ of the year is January.

My baby sister now has three _____.

When my first _____ fell out, I got ten cents.

I am going shopping _____ Mum after school tomorrow.

The _____ was flying around the bright light.

2 Use these clues to write –th words.

a large container for washing yourself in _____

an opening in your face _____

a part of the year _____

material for making clothes _____

an insect like a butterfly _____

3 Finish the words below the pictures.

b a _ _ _

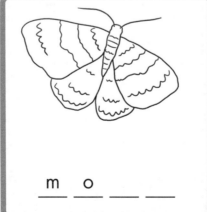

m o _ _ _

t o o _ _

4 Use these list words in sentences of your own.

tooth _____

bath _____

both _____

cloth _____

mouth _____

5 Fill the gaps in the **–th** list words as you go along the path.

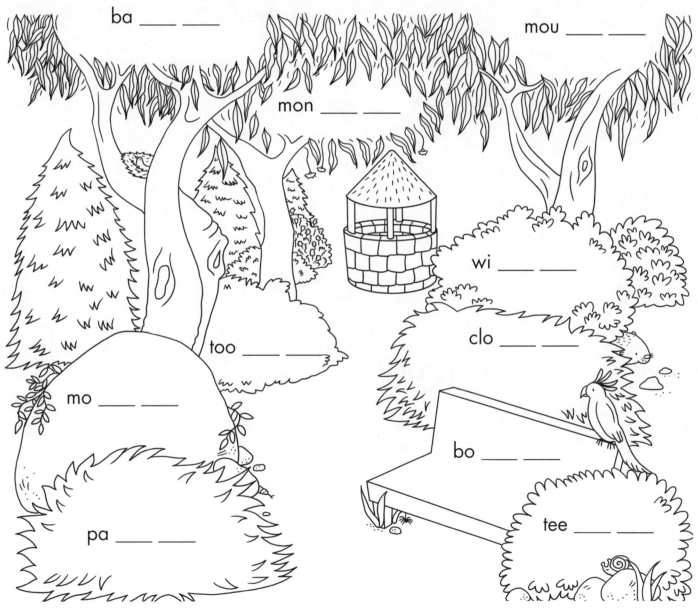

ba ___ ___

mou ___ ___

mon ___ ___

wi ___ ___

clo ___ ___

too ___ ___

mo ___ ___

bo ___ ___

pa ___ ___

tee ___ ___

More –nk words

stink	bunk	trunk	junk	plank
blink	sunk	skunk	dunk	blank

1 Choose a list word to finish each sentence.

The _____ is a strange animal.

Snakes do not have eyelids, so they cannot _____.

A _____ is a wooden ship used in China.

Mahmet fell out of his _____ last night.

The pirates made the sailor walk the _____.

2 Use these groups of letters to write –nk words.

du

bla

tru   **nk**

su

sti

3 Draw three trunks!

A trunk for putting clothes in	An elephant's trunk	A tree trunk

4 Use these clues to write –nk words.

a long flat piece of wood   _____

not filled in   _____

a very strong, bad smell   _____

the wooden stem of a tree   _____

open and close your eyes quickly   _____

5 Fill the trunk with –nk words. Use these sounds to help you.

bla   su   bli   sti   sku   du

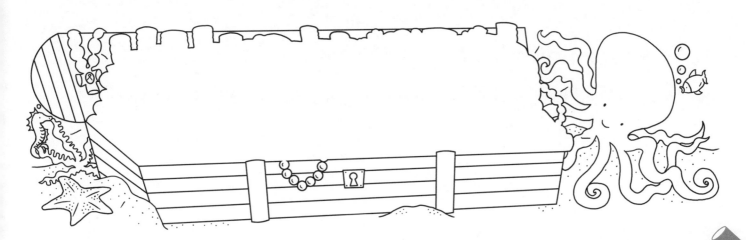

ee words

weed	meet	weep	deep	sleep	sheep
feed	seen	peep	keep	tree	green

1 Follow the **ee** pattern to make words that rhyme with weed, meet and weep.

weed

f ____ ____ d

r ____ ____ d

bl ____ ____ d

n ____ ____ d

sp ____ ____ d

d ____ ____ d

br ____ ____ d

s ____ ____ d

meet

f ____ ____ t

sw ____ ____ t

fl ____ ____ t

b ____ ____ t

gr ____ ____ t

sh ____ ____ t

sl ____ ____ t

str ____ ____ t

weep

d ____ ____ p

p ____ ____ p

k ____ ____ p

sl ____ ____ p

sh ____ ____ p

st ____ ____ p

cr ____ ____ p

sw ____ ____ p

2 Put circles around the correct words in the brackets.

Little Bo Peep has lost her (sleep, sheep).

There is a large (tree, keep) in our back garden.

Have you (seen, keen) Carmel's new game?

I was so tired I went to (peep, sleep) in the chair.

When David brought home a stray dog, his dad said he could not
(deep, keep) it.

26

3 Read the words, write them down and draw pictures to match them.

A woolly sheep	A shady tree	A green jumper
_____ _____	_____ _____	_____ _____

4 Use these list words in sentences of your own.

weed _____

seen _____

weep _____

5 Add **ing** to each of these words and then read the new words aloud.

sleep ____ ____ ____   meet ____ ____ ____   weed ____ ____ ____

Now use them in sentences of your own.

sleeping _____

meeting _____

weeding _____

Challenge words				
sneeze	kneel	between	screen	toffee
squeeze	needle	steep	breeze	cheese

ai words

pain	rain	brain	grain	snail
main	drain	stain	nail	pail

1 Choose a list word to finish each sentence.

Kerry had a big red _____ on her new white jumper.

The _____ was eating our lettuce leaves.

Peter was in a lot of _____ when he cut his finger.

Jack and Jill went up the hill to fetch a _____ of water.

The road flooded when the _____ was blocked.

2 Follow the **ai** pattern to make words that rhyme with pain and nail.

pain   **nail**

m ___ ___ n   r ___ ___ n   sn ___ ___ l   p ___ ___ l

dr ___ ___ n   br ___ ___ n   r ___ ___ l   fr ___ ___ l

st ___ ___ n   gr ___ ___ n   h ___ ___ l   m ___ ___ l

g ___ ___ n   v ___ ___ n   s ___ ___ l   t ___ ___ l

pl ___ ___ n   str ___ ___ n   w ___ ___ l   tr ___ ___ l

tr ___ ___ n   rem ___ ___ n   f ___ ___ l   qu ___ ___ l

3 Unjumble these **ai** words.

nairg   lsnai   rnbai

_____   _____   _____

4 Use these clues to write **ai** words.

the seed of wheat, corn, oats, etc.   ___ ___ ___ ___ ___

a pipe for taking away unwanted water   ___ ___ ___ ___ ___

drops of water from clouds in the sky   ___ ___ ___ ___

a dirty mark on something   ___ ___ ___ ___ ___

the feeling you have when you are hurt   ___ ___ ___ ___

5 Fill the snail with **ai** words.

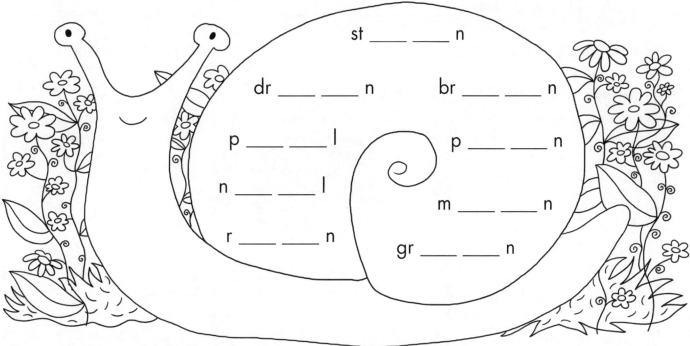

st ___ ___ n

dr ___ ___ n   br ___ ___ n

p ___ ___ l   p ___ ___ n

n ___ ___ l

m ___ ___ n

r ___ ___ n   gr ___ ___ n

6 Finish the words below the pictures.

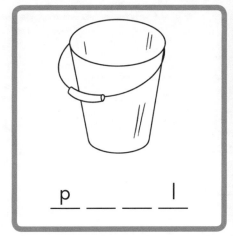

p ___ ___ l

r ___ ___ n

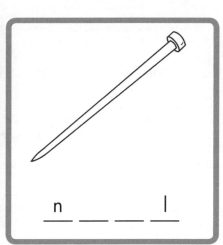

n ___ ___ l

ea words

clean	lean	cream	leaf	head
mean	bean	dream	bread	dead

1 Choose a list word to finish each sentence.

Mum likes lots of _____ on her strawberries.

Harry put on a _____ shirt to go to the party.

The autumn _____ was a lovely red colour.

Last night I had a scary _____.

The smell from the hot _____ shop made me feel hungry.

2 Finish the words below the pictures.

__ __ a __

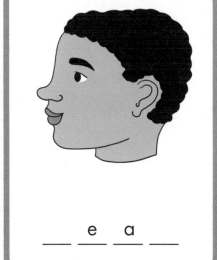

__ __ a __

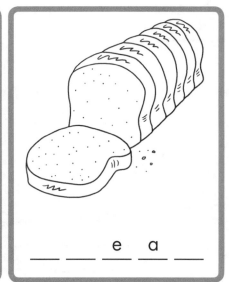

__ __ a __

3 Write two words that rhyme with each of the words below.

steam   _____   _____

mean   _____   _____

head   _____   _____

4 Acrosswords: use the clues below to find the words.

a | | e | a | |

d | | e | a | |

b | | | e | a | |

e | | | e | a | |

c | | e | a | |

a The flat green part of a plant or tree

b Food made mostly of flour and baked in an oven

c A vegetable with large seeds, which can be cooked and eaten

d Not alive

e The thick part of milk

5 Which **ea** word from the list could fit into both these sentences?

You were _____ to hide her toys.

I didn't _____ to come home late.

6 Use these letters to make as many **ea** words as you can.

br m cr
cl f
l — **ea** — n
d dr
b t h

_____ _____ _____

_____ _____ _____

_____ _____ _____

_____ _____ _____

_____ _____ _____

7 Circle the **ea** words in these columns.

clean	coal	slow	scale	first	cream	head
raid	foal	dream	alive	lean	name	dead
mean	leaf	bread	alone	bean	trace	beam

Book Week words

book	page	write	award	illustrate
read	story	author	publish	cover

1 Use these list words in sentences of your own.

write _____

story _____

author _____

read _____

cover _____

2 Finish these sentences.

The last book I read was _____ .

My favourite book is _____ .

The author is _____ .

I like it because _____ .

On the front cover is _____ .

3 Fill in the book pages with list words.

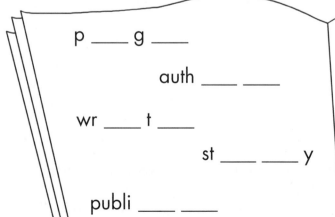

p ___ g ___

auth ___ ___

wr ___ t ___

st ___ ___ y

publi ___ ___

aw ___ ___ d

cov ___ ___

r ___ ___ d

illustr ___ t ___

b ___ ___ k

4 Use these clues to write Book Week words.

a prize for doing something well   __ __ __ __ __

someone who writes stories and poems   __ __ __ __ __ __

an adventure told or written   __ __ __ __ __

one side of a sheet of paper   __ __ __ __

draw pictures for a book   __ __ __ __ __ __ __ __ __

5 Can you find these Book Week words in the grid below?

| write | page | story | award | book | cover |

The words go either across or down.

r	a	e	d	p	c	b
e	w	r	i	a	o	o
a	a	u	t	g	v	o
w	r	i	t	e	e	k
m	d	s	t	o	r	y

6 Mind your Ps and Qs! Cross out all the Ps and Qs in the grid to find some Book Week words.

p	a	u	q	t	h	o	r
a	p	w	a	q	r	p	d
q	c	o	v	e	p	q	r
w	p	r	i	p	q	t	e
q	s	t	p	o	p	r	y

_____

_____

_____

_____

_____

More **ea** words

tea	heat	wheat	real	meal
read	neat	please	seal	heal

1 Choose a list word to finish each sentence.

The _____ from the sun can burn your skin.

May I have a drink, _____ ?

The first _____ of the day is breakfast.

Jenny's writing is very _____.

The sore on my hand is starting to _____.

2 Use these letters to make as many **ea** words as you can.

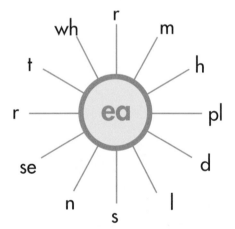

_____ _____ _____

_____ _____ _____

_____ _____ _____

_____ _____ _____

_____ _____

3 Read the words, write them down and draw pictures to match them.

A field of wheat	My favourite meal	A cup of tea
_____	_____	_____
_____	_____	_____

4 Put a circle around the correct words in the brackets.

The farmer planted a crop of (wheat, heat).

With my breakfast I had a cup of (real, tea).

Dinner is my favourite (meal, real) of the day.

I (read, please) some of my book every night.

You look very (heat, neat) today.

5 Complete the **ea** words in the balls.

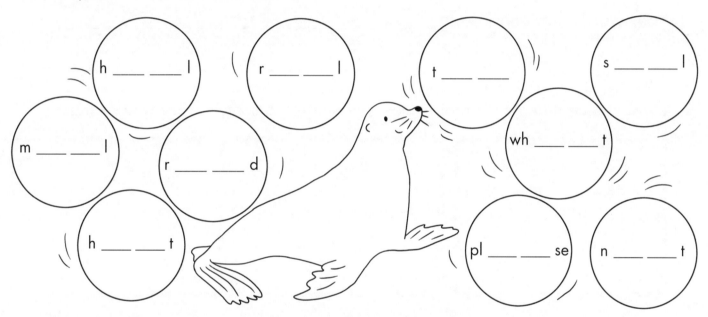

h ___ ___ l

r ___ ___ l

t ___ ___ ___

s ___ ___ l

m ___ ___ l

r ___ ___ d

wh ___ ___ t

h ___ ___ t

pl ___ ___ se

n ___ ___ t

6 Which **ea** list word could fit into both these sentences?

Mum had to _____ the bag of corn before putting it into the freezer.

The _____ swam around in the icy water.

-ng words

sang	rang	fang	gang	along
song	rung	thong	wrong	lung

1 Use list words to complete the following.

Four words that end in **ong**   _____   _____

_____   _____

Two words that end in **ung**   _____   _____

Four words that end in **ang**   _____   _____

_____   _____

2 Draw a blue thong on a foot, a pop star singing a song, and a wolf's fang.

3 Which list words go with the other words?

group	crowd	troop	_____
shoe	sandal	sneaker	_____
bad	evil	false	_____
body	heart	breathe	_____

4 Write these letters in alphabetical order.

r   a   s   f   _____

Now write these words in alphabetical order.

sang   fang   along   rang

_____

5 Write the list word that goes with each picture.

_ _ _ _ _   _ _ _ _ _   _ _ _ _ _ _ _

6 Use these list words to fill the gaps in the sentences.

sang   song   rang   rung

Jordyn _____ at the Christmas concert.

My favourite _____ is an old one called *Mamma Mia*.

Millie _____ the bell when it was time for lunch.

I have _____ home three
    times but no one is answering the phone.

Did you know?

The step on a ladder is called a rung.

7 Use list words to answer the following.

music for the voice   _____

a group of people together   _____

part of the body that helps us breathe   _____

a long, sharp tooth   _____

a flat shoe worn in summer   _____

Essential words 2

because	did	wish	what	have	house
very	just	like	make	more	other

1 Underline all the list words you can find in these sentences.

When you blew out your birthday candles, what did you wish for?

Our house is just like any other house in our street.

I will have to make some more cup cakes because you have eaten all
the others.

2 Use these list words in sentences of your own.

very _____

because _____

more _____

other _____

did _____

3 Unjumble these list words.

kema   ohsue

_____   _____

yrev   tsju

_____   _____

herto   cueeabs

_____   _____

4 Write a story about a snail using as many of the list words as you can.

_____

_____

_____

_____

5 Complete these boxes to make words from the list.

	i		e

		s	h

	a		e

	e	r	

w	h		

		s	t

6 Put the missing vowels in each of these list words.

b ____ c ____ ____ s ____   ____ th ____ r   d ____ d

m ____ r ____   w ____ sh   wh ____ t

h ____ ____ s ____   j ____ st   v ____ ry

7 Answer these questions about the list words.

Which word has four letters and rhymes with dish?   _____

Which word has five letters and rhymes with mouse?   _____

Which word has four letters and rhymes with sore?   _____

Which word has three letters and rhymes with hid?   _____

Can you think of a word that rhymes with very?   _____

Revision

1 Place these words in the correct balloons.

cloth	grain	wheat	tooth	please	bread	snail
song	stain	lung	wrong	month	mouth	gang
sleep	dream	keep	sheep	drain	green	

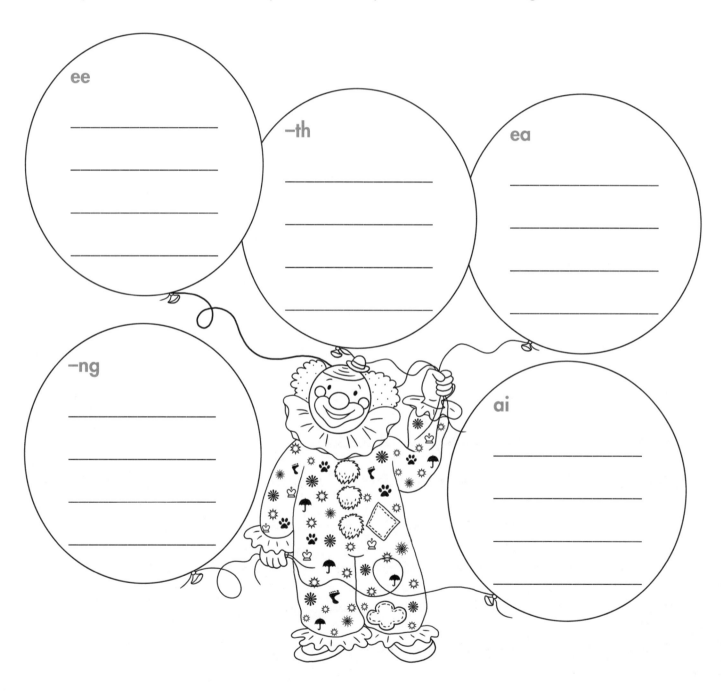

ee

–th

ea

–ng

ai

2 Use the words below to label the scene. Then colour the picture.

leaf   snail   rain   moth   junk   path   weed   bath

pail   tree   plank   nail   skunk   drain   thong

ing words

king	wing	sting	string	spring	singlet
ring	swing	fling	cling	wring	ringlet
sing	thing	bring	sling	single	jingle

1 Choose a list word to finish each sentence.

Mary is going to _____ her pet lamb to school tomorrow.

The _____ and queen rode in the carriage.

If you annoy that insect, it will _____ you.

The toy car wouldn't go because the _____ was broken.

The shearer was wearing a blue _____.

2 Add **ing** to each of these words, then read the new words aloud.

ring ____ ____ ____   sing ____ ____ ____   swing ____ ____ ____

Now use them in sentences of your own.

ringing _____

singing _____

swinging _____

3 Find list words to match these patterns.

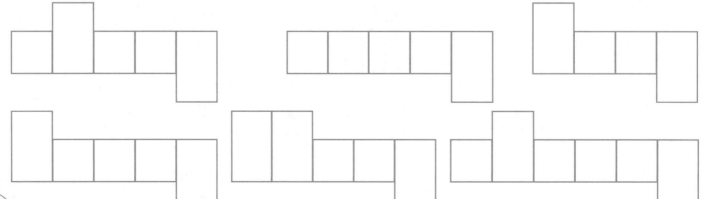

4 Which **ing** list word could fit into both these sentences?

Jan had a gold _____ on her third finger.

We could hear the bell _____ as we ran to school.

5 Use these list words in sentences of your own.

thing _____

wing _____

sling _____

swing _____

ringlet _____

wring _____

jingle _____

6 Read the words, write them down and draw pictures to match them.

A fat king	A string bag	A ring on a finger
_____	_____	_____
_____	_____	_____

—ear words

ear	near	clear	tear	shear
dear	hear	fear	gear	spear

1 Choose a list word to finish each sentence.

At the show we saw a man _____ some sheep.

The hunter threw the _____ at the wild animal.

My cousin lives _____ the football ground.

I could _____ the tap dripping all night.

Barry does not like spiders, but I have no _____ of them.

2 Use these list words in sentences of your own.

ear _____

clear _____

dear _____

tear _____

gear _____

3 Circle the —ear words in these columns.

deal	fear	shear	gear	dear	hear
leader	tear	near	spear	seal	peach
maid	round	teach	dream	grain	clear

4 **Acrosswords**: use the clues below to finish the words.

a [ ][ ] e a r   **d** [ ] e a r

b [ ][ ] e a r   **e** [ ][ ] e a r

c [ ] e a r

a Easy to understand, see or hear

b Cut the wool off an animal

c Not far away

d Listen to sounds

e A long pole with a very sharp point

5 When tear rhymes with near, it means a drop of water that comes out of your eye when you cry.

When tear rhymes with wear, it means to rip.

Use tear in these sentences.

The _____ rolled down the sad boy's face.

Look at the _____ in my coat.

Challenge words

| nose | sail | hole | wore | brake |
| knows | sale | whole | war | break |

45

a–e words

cake	make	stake	name	mate	shade
take	rake	shake	game	made	spade

1 Write two list words that rhyme with each of the words below.

take _____ _____

same _____ _____

made _____ _____

2 Choose a list word to finish each sentence.

I helped Mum _____ up all the autumn leaves.

Peter was so cold that he started to _____.

My favourite board _____ is Snakes and Ladders.

On hot days I always play in the _____.

Uncle Jim says you should always buy things that are _____
in Australia.

3 Read the words, write them down and draw pictures to match them.

My best mate	A birthday cake	A garden rake
_____	_____	_____
_____	_____	_____

4 Use the letters in the two columns to make as many a–e words as you can.

| c |
| t |
| st |
| m |
| r |
| sp |
| sh |
| n |
| g |

+ a +

| k |
| m |
| t |
| d |

+ e

_____ _____ _____

_____ _____ _____

_____ _____ _____

_____ _____ _____

_____ _____ _____

5 Fill in the following a–e words.

g ___ m ___   sh ___ k ___   n ___ m ___   r ___ k ___

sh ___ d ___   m ___ d ___   m ___ k ___   t ___ k ___

c ___ k ___   st ___ k ___   m ___ t ___   sp ___ d ___

6 Follow the a–e pattern to make words that rhyme with cake, name and mate.

cake

t ___ k ___

r ___ k ___

st ___ k ___

sh ___ k ___

sn ___ k ___

l ___ k ___

w ___ k ___

br ___ k ___

name

g ___ m ___

t ___ m ___

bl ___ m ___

l ___ m ___

c ___ m ___

f ___ m ___

s ___ m ___

fr ___ m ___

mate

___ t ___

g ___ t ___

l ___ t ___

d ___ t ___

r ___ t ___

h ___ t ___

sl ___ t ___

pl ___ t ___

47

More a–e words

came	blame	wake	lake	whale	stale
same	lame	bake	safe	sale	cage

1 Write two list words that rhyme with each of the words below.

same _____ _____

bake _____ _____

sale _____ _____

2 Choose a list word to finish each sentence.

The _____ was swimming close to the shore.

The tiger looked very unhappy in the _____.

Don't _____ me for breaking the glass.

The horse was _____ and couldn't run.

The explorers camped beside the _____ .

3 Which a–e word could fit into both of these sentences?

The money was put into the large steel _____.

I feel _____ at night if the light is on.

4 Finish the words below the pictures.

c ___ g ____   wh ___ l ___   s ___ f ___

5 **Acrosswords**: use the clues below to finish these list words.

a

d

b

e

c

a Not fresh; made a long time ago

b A huge sea animal

c Say someone made something bad happen

d A special time when things are sold at lower prices

e Not able to walk properly because of a sore leg or foot

6 Fill the safe with **a–e** words.

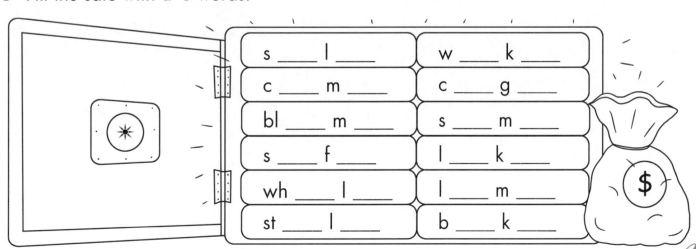

s ___ l ___   w ___ k ___
c ___ m ___   c ___ g ___
bl ___ m ___   s ___ m ___
s ___ f ___   l ___ k ___
wh ___ l ___   l ___ m ___
st ___ l ___   b ___ k ___

49

o–e words

nose	bone	hole	smoke	woke	joke	choke
rose	cone	note	alone	spoke	poke	slope
hose	pole	broke	stone	rope	stroke	

1 Choose a list word to finish each sentence.

Laksmir planted a beautiful white _____.

A rabbit's _____ is called a burrow.

On hot days I run under the _____.

Lee had an ice-cream _____.

I was upset when my new toy _____.

I like to _____ my cat's fur.

It was hard running down the _____.

2 Follow the o–e pattern to make words that rhyme with broke, nose and bone.

broke

sm ___ k ___   p ___ k ___

c ___ k ___   br ___ k ___

str ___ k ___   w ___ k ___

sp ___ k ___

ch ___ k ___

j ___ k ___

nose

r ___ s ___

h ___ s ___

cl ___ s ___

ch ___ s ___

th ___ s ___

p ___ s ___

bone

c ___ n ___

t ___ n ___

teleph ___ n ___

z ___ n ___

al ___ n ___

st ___ n ___

3 Use the letters in the two columns to make as many o–e words as you can.

br
n
b
sm
c
r
h
p

+ o +

k
n
s
l
t

+ e

_____ _____ _____

_____ _____ _____

_____ _____ _____

_____ _____ _____

_____ _____ _____

4 **Acrosswords**: use the clues below to finish these list words.

a | | | o | | e |

d | | o | | e |

b | | o | | e |

e | | o | | e |

c | | | o | | e |

a Blue or grey gas that floats up from a fire

b A short letter or message

c When you are by yourself

d One of the hard, white pieces of your body that make up your skeleton

e A long rubber tube that water can go through

5 Finish the words below the pictures.

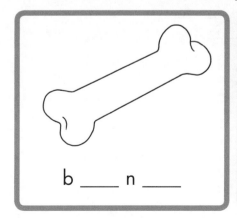

b ____ n ____

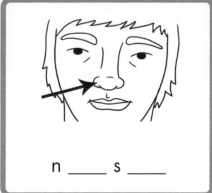

n ____ s ____

r ____ s ____

or words

sort	sport	corn	horn	pork
fort	torn	born	cork	fork

1 Write two list words that rhyme with each of the words below.

sort _____ _____

corn _____ _____

pork _____ _____

2 Choose a list word to finish each sentence.

Dad took the _____ out of the bottle.

I was _____ at Mildura hospital.

The corner of this page is _____.

_____ is meat that comes from a pig.

Jenny loves to play _____, but Tam prefers to read.

3 Use these letters to make as many **or** words as you can.

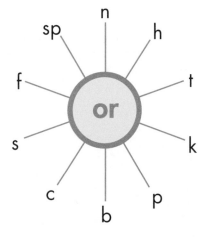

_____ _____ _____

_____ _____ _____

_____ _____

_____ _____

_____ _____

4 Unjumble these **or** words.

orhn   ports   orcn

_____   _____   _____

5 Use these list words in sentences of your own.

fort _____

corn _____

sport _____

sort _____

fork _____

6 Can you find these **or** words in the grid below?

| sort | fork | torn | sport | horn | corn | cork |

The words go either across or down.

c	o	r	n	o	r	s
o	f	s	p	o	r	t
r	f	o	r	k	b	o
k	a	r	e	c	o	r
r	e	t	h	o	r	n

7 Find **or** list words to match these patterns.

Challenge words

| report | actor | north | shore | sailor |
| torch | inventor | monitor | doctor | horror |

ow words

low	show	flow	own	blown	below	window
bow	snow	follow	tow	grow	elbow	throw
slow	crow	bowl	blow	grown	shown	

1 Choose a list word to finish each sentence.

A tortoise is a _____ animal.

Gwenda has a red _____ in her hair.

If you go first, I will _____ you.

It is fun playing in the _____, but it gets very cold.

I had a _____ of soup when I came home from netball.

2 Use these list words in sentences of your own.

own _____

crow _____

elbow _____

show _____

blown _____

3 When bow rhymes with low, it means a knot with two loops and two ends.

When bow rhymes with now, it means to bend your body or head forward.

Put bow into these sentences.

The _____ on your shoelace is undone.

When the queen arrives, we will _____ to her.

54

4 Add **ing** to each of these words, then read the new words aloud.

show ____ ____ ____   snow ____ ____ ____   follow ____ ____ ____

Now use them in sentences of your own.

showing   _____

snowing   _____

following   _____

5 Can you find these **ow** words in the grid below?

| own | snow | slow | low | flow | bowl | crow | show | bow |

The words go either
across or down.

s	l	o	w	e	b	a
h	o	s	c	r	o	w
o	w	n	o	t	w	o
w	n	o	f	l	o	w
b	o	w	l	a	m	p

6 Change letters to make new words.

Change one letter in low to make a thick, round
    piece of wood.   ____ ____ ____

Change one letter in crow to make a word meaning
    to become bigger.   ____ ____ ____ ____

Change one letter in slow to make a word meaning
    to move along smoothly, like a river.   ____ ____ ____ ____

Change one letter in own to make a bird that comes
    out at night.   ____ ____ ____

i–e words

ice	nice	ripe	white	kite
mice	rice	wipe	write	bike

1 Write two list words that rhyme with each of the words below.

rice _____ _____

pipe _____ _____

write _____ _____

2 Choose a list word to finish each sentence.

Ming has three _____ in a cage.

There was not enough wind to fly our _____.

Tonight I will _____ a letter to my aunt in Dunedin.

The fruit fell off the tree when it was _____.

The penguin slid on the _____.

3 Use these list words in sentences of your own.

white _____

nice _____

wipe _____

rice _____

bike _____

ice _____

write _____

4 Read the words, write them down and draw pictures to match them.

A red kite	Three white mice	A new bike
_____	_____	_____
_____	_____	_____

5 Fill in the blanks to make **i–e** words.

b ____ k ____   r ____ c ____   m ____ c ____

r ____ p ____   w ____ p ____   wh ____ t ____

____ c ____   k ____ t ____   wr ____ t ____

n ____ c ____

6 What are we? We are words that rhyme with nice.

We are small furry animals.   ___ ___ ___ ___

We are white grains used as a food.   ___ ___ ___ ___

I am water made hard by the cold.   ___ ___ ___

7 Find list words to match these patterns.

Sports words

netball	hockey	swimming	diving	cricket
football	running	basketball	tennis	jumping

1 Use list words to complete the following.

Three words that end with ball _____ _____

_____

Two words that have **ck** in them _____ _____

Four words that end in **ing** _____ _____

_____ _____

2 Draw a swimming pool, a tennis racquet and a pair of football boots.

3 Try to match these football games with the clues.

soccer   rugby union   Australian Rules   gridiron

This football game is played mainly in the United States. _____

This football game uses a round ball. _____

This football game is played in many countries and
    you can run with the ball. _____

This football game is played mainly in Australia and
    you catch, kick or punch the ball. _____

4 Write these letters in alphabetical order.

h   f   c   t   _____

Now write these words in alphabetical order.

tennis   football   hockey   cricket

_____

5 Write the list word that goes which each picture.

‒ ‒ ‒ ‒ ‒ ‒ ‒   ‒ ‒ ‒ ‒ ‒ ‒ ‒   ‒ ‒ ‒ ‒ ‒ ‒ ‒

6 Use the given word to finish each sentence.

swimmer   The _____ had to get up very early in the

morning to go to training.

jumped   The bar was very high but I _____ over it.

netballer   After the game the _____ was very tired.

dove   Paige stood on the diving board and _____ into

the water.

| Did you know? |

Cricket as a sport was first played more than 500 years ago. Another type of cricket is an insect that makes a lot of noise by rubbing its front wings together.

Revision

1 Place these words in the correct balloons.

stake	shade	follow	sport	bring	sort	thing
broke	snow	corn	crow	own	smoke	spade
sting	game	hole	swing	rose	cork	

–ing
_____
_____
_____

a–e
_____
_____
_____

or
_____
_____
_____

o–e
_____
_____
_____

ow
_____
_____
_____

2 In these boxes, finish the words and match them with pictures, or write words to match the drawings.

__ __ __ __ __	b __ __ l	__ __ __ __
c __ g __	__ __ __ __	c __ __ w
__ __ __ __	b __ k __	__ __ __ __
sp __ d __	__ __ __ __ __	n __ s __

More i–e words

side	wide	tide	time	nine
ride	hide	slide	shine	mine

1 Write two list words to rhyme with each word below.

wide _____ _____

nine _____ _____

2 Choose a list word to finish each sentence.

I had a _____ on a tram when I was in Melbourne.

Matt went down the big _____.

What is the _____, please?

Is it _____ o'clock yet?

Most of the sand was covered with water when the _____

came in.

3 Circle the i–e words in these columns.

clean	slide	long	shake
time	swing	shine	ride
game	think	smoke	luck
broke	hide	rose	blame
mice	thick	white	tide

4 Find list words to match these patterns.

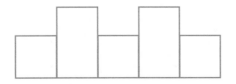  

5 Follow the **i–e** pattern to make words that rhyme with side, time and shine.

side	time	shine
r ___ d ___	l ___ m ___	n ___ n ___
w ___ d ___	m ___ m ___	m ___ n ___
h ___ d ___	ch ___ m ___	l ___ n ___
t ___ d ___	cr ___ m ___	f ___ n ___
sl ___ d ___	sl ___ m ___	p ___ n ___
pr ___ d ___		d ___ n ___
br ___ d ___		

6 Can you find these list words in the grid below?

slide	shine	side
ride	hide	wide
nine	tide	time

The words go either across or down.

c	a	r	t	s	t	y
s	h	i	n	e	i	e
l	i	d	i	w	d	t
i	d	e	n	i	e	i
d	e	n	e	d	e	m
e	s	i	d	e	p	e

Challenge words

knife	invite	strike	stripe	slice
exercise	twice	prize	crime	missile

oa words

coat	soak	coast	toad	foal	coach	float
boat	oats	roast	foam	moan	croak	groan
oak	toast	loaf	goal	goat	throat	

1 Choose a list word to finish each sentence.

Acorns come from _____ trees.

Tonight we are having _____ beef for dinner.

A _____ is like a frog.

Adam likes jam on his _____.

Mandy gave the horse some _____.

2 Use these list words in sentences of your own.

soak _____

foam _____

loaf _____

croak _____

3 Add the letter **s** to make these words plural.

toad ____   boat ____   coat ____   foal ____   goat ____

4 Unjumble these **oa** words.

soact   oamn   soat

_____   _____   _____

oatd   hrttoa

_____   _____

5 Add **ing** to each of these words, then read the new words aloud.

soak ____ ____ ____   toast ____ ____ ____   roast ____ ____ ____

Now use them in sentences of your own.

soaking _____

toasting _____

roasting _____

6 Fill the loaf of bread with **oa** words. Use the letters to help you.

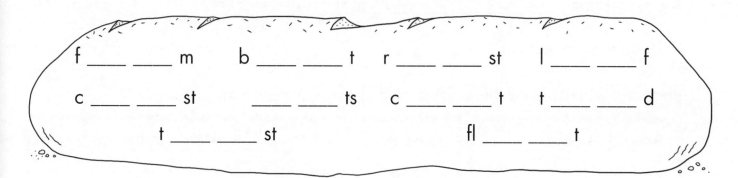

f ____ ____ m   b ____ ____ t   r ____ ____ st   l ____ ____ f

c ____ ____ st   ____ ____ ts   c ____ ____ t   t ____ ____ d

t ____ ____ st   fl ____ ____ t

7 Finish these words by adding **oa**. Match the words to the pictures.

t ____ ____ d

t ____ ____ st

c ____ ____ t

l ____ ____ f

b ____ ____ t

ur words

turn	curl	burst	nurse	church
burn	hurt	fur	surf	purse

1 Choose a list word to finish each sentence.

When I was in hospital, the _____ was very nice.

Our _____ has a large cross on the roof.

If you play with matches you will _____ yourself.

Mum lost her _____ at the supermarket.

A bear is covered with _____.

2 Read the words, write them down and draw pictures to match them.

An old church	Wild surf	A kind nurse
_____	_____	_____
_____	_____	_____

3 Add **ing** to each of these words, then read the new words aloud.

burn ____ ____ ____   hurt ____ ____ ____   turn ____ ____ ____

Now use them in sentences of your own.

burning _____

hurting _____

turning _____

4 Circle the **ur** words in these columns.

nurse	dream	burst	towel	burn
hunt	surf	sport	start	blunt
church	author	follow	turn	curl
purse	shear	fur	count	hurt

5 Find list words to match these patterns.

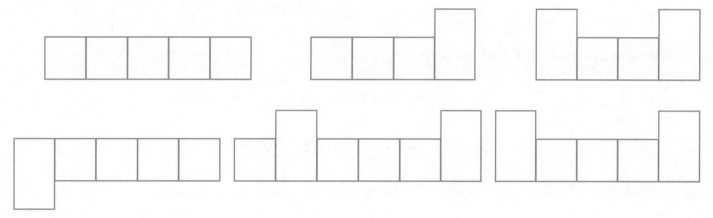

6 Use these letters to write **ur** words.

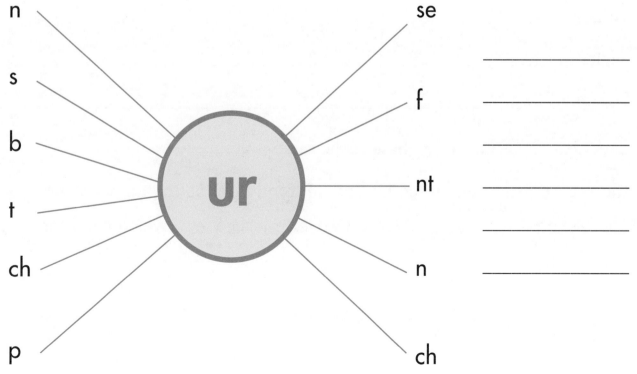

er words

over	supper	summer	fern	letter	water	spider
under	later	farmer	other	better	silver	teacher
never	winter	Easter	river	thunder	corner	

1 Choose a list word to finish each sentence.

The small insect crawled _____ the rock.

The _____ spun a web in the barn.

We have hot cross buns during _____.

The _____ planted the wheat in the fields.

Sometimes in _____ it gets very hot.

2 Use these words in sentences of your own.

over _____

never _____

supper _____

winter _____

fern _____

3 Underline any list words in these sentences.

The snail crawled under the leaf of the fern to get out of the hot summer sun.

Later, when it was cooler, it crawled over a lettuce leaf, which it ate for supper.

4 Find the list words to match these patterns.

5 Can you find these **er** words in the grid below?

| never | over | Easter | under | fern | farmer | later |

f	f	o	l	l	o	w
e	a	s	t	e	r	a
r	r	u	n	d	e	r
n	m	l	a	t	e	r
n	e	v	e	r	a	t
c	r	o	v	e	r	s

The words go either across or down.

6 Find the list words described below.

the coldest season of the year   __ __ __ __ __ __

a green, leafy plant that grows in damp places   __ __ __ __

a loud noise during storms   __ __ __ __ __ __ __

beneath or below   __ __ __ __ __

a drink from taps   __ __ __ __ __

Double consonants

letter	butter	puddle	paddle	ribbon
better	cuddle	middle	summer	rubber

1 Choose a list word to finish each sentence.

Dot's dress was wet after she fell in the _____.

Kim tied red _____ around the present.

A car tyre is made from _____.

The _____ part of an apple is called the core.

_____ is made from milk.

2 Which three list words match this pattern?

_____

_____

_____

Which two list words match this pattern?

_____

_____

Which two list words match this pattern?

_____

_____

Which two list words match this pattern?

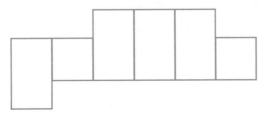

_____

_____

3 Unjumble these list words.

laddpe   niorbb   dducel

_____   _____   _____

4 Put circles around the correct words in the brackets.

Tayla put some (better, butter) on her toast.

In (middle, summer) I like to go swimming.

Yesterday I posted a (letter, better) to my grandfather.

My little brother can't swim, but he likes to (paddle, puddle).

I woke up in the (cuddle, middle) of the night.

5 Finish the words below the pictures.

__ __ dd __ __

__ __ bb __ __

__ __ tt __ __

Tom and Clare Smith
18 Jones Street
Springtown   1234

Challenge words

ad**d**ress	kennel	collapse	puzzle	tunnel
forgo**tt**en	i**ll**ness	collect	traffic	collar

More double consonants

| dinner | happy | stiff | puff | shell |
| winner | off | cliff | sell | spell |

1 Choose a list word to finish each sentence.

Joe was sore when he fell _____ the chair.

Slowly the man climbed up the _____.

Anna was the _____ of the first race.

Ali was very _____ when she won the prize.

Levi has a large _____ collection.

2 Use these list words in sentences of your own.

dinner _____

spell _____

puff _____

stiff _____

sell _____

3 Unjumble these list words.

ffup _____   llesh _____   sifft _____

hyppa _____   rwienn _____   eplls _____

4 Can you find these list words in the grid below?

The words go either across or down.

winner	sell
spell	off
cliff	shell
dinner	

s	o	l	d	o	g	o
h	c	l	i	f	f	f
e	s	t	n	i	s	f
l	w	i	n	n	e	r
l	s	p	e	l	l	o
p	c	a	r	t	l	m

5 Put circles around the correct words in the brackets.

The witch cast a magic (spell, shell).

A crab has a hard (spell, shell).

I hope Dad has cooked a chicken for (dinner, winner) tonight.

The old paintbrush was (stiff, cliff).

6 Finish the words below the pictures.

_ _ _ ll

_ _ nn _ _

_ _ _ ff

7 Which list word can fit into both these sentences?

I can _____ all the words in this book.

The frog changed into a prince when the _____ was broken.

ou words

shout	trout	found	round	cloud
pouch	south	ground	about	mouse

1 Use list words to complete the following.

Three words that end in **t** _____ _____

_____

Four words that end in **d** _____ _____

_____ _____

Three other words _____ _____

_____

2 Draw a round basketball, a furry grey mouse, and the sun peeping from behind a cloud.

3 Which list words go with the other words?

bream   carp   perch   _____

earth   soil   dirt   _____

yellscream   noise   _____

bag   pocket   purse   _____

4 Write these letters in alphabetical order.

   p   s   f   a   _____

74

Now write these words in alphabetical order.

found   south   about   pouch

_____

5 Write the list word that goes with each picture.

_ _ _ _ _	_ _ _ _ _	_ _ _ _ _

6 Look how the list word has been changed. Use the new word to complete the sentence.

shouting   Billy was _____ so much at the football match

             that he nearly lost his voice.

cloudy   It was sunny this morning but now it is _____.

mice   There were three _____ in the farmer's barn.

7 Use these clues to write list words.

nearly or around   _____

the opposite of north   _____

the earth or land   _____

a freshwater fish   _____

Did you know?

The word ground can also mean having been crushed to powder. Ground coffee, for example, is where coffee beans have been crushed into a powder.

Space words

| space | moon | comet | planet | rocket |
| sun | star | craft | Earth | Solar System |

1 Use the given list words to complete these sentences.

planet   A _____ is a heavenly body that moves around

the sun.

sun   The _____ gives heat and light to the Earth.

Earth   The planet we live on is called _____ .

comet   A _____ is a star-like body with a tail of light.

star   In the night sky a _____ looks like a point of light.

moon   The heavenly body that moves around the Earth is called the

_____ .

2 Draw a rocket, a cow jumping over the moon and a bright star.

3 Write these letters in alphabetical order.

m   c   r   p   s   _____

Now write these words in alphabetical order.

rocket   star   craft   moon   planet

_____

4 Can you find these list words in the grid below?

craft	star
comet	space
sun	moon
rocket	

s	p	a	c	e	z	c
u	m	o	o	n	o	r
n	e	a	m	o	p	a
r	t	h	e	a	r	f
r	o	s	t	a	r	t
r	o	c	k	e	t	a

The words go either across or down.

5 Find list words that rhyme with these words.

spoon _____   far _____

won _____   socket _____

place _____   raft _____

6 Unjumble these list words.

nus _____   trcaf _____

aoSlr esyStm _____   tealpn _____

tecork _____   teocm _____

7 Here are some more space words.

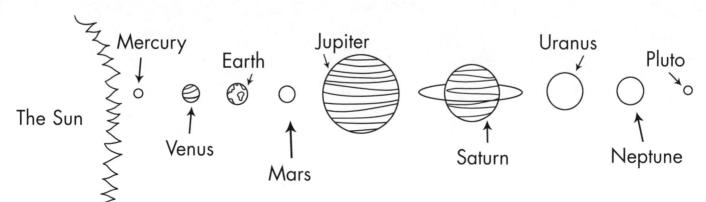

The Sun   Mercury   Venus   Earth   Mars   Jupiter   Saturn   Uranus   Neptune   Pluto

Holiday words

| caravan | travel | fishing | swimming | outback |
| sunshine | houseboat | aeroplane | beach | pool |

1 Use list words to complete the following.

Three words with seven letters _____ _____

_____

Two words with nine letters _____ _____

The shortest word _____

2 Draw an aeroplane, a caravan and a person fishing.

3 Which list words go with the other words?

car	towing	park	_____
rod	tackle	line	_____
dry	dusty	kangaroos	_____
sunhat	sunglasses	sunscreen	_____

4 Write these letters in alphabetical order.

p   h   t   b   _____

Now write these words in alphabetical order.

houseboat   travel   pool   beach

5 Write the list word that goes with each picture.

_ _ _ _ _ _ _

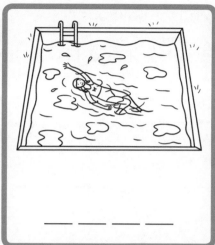

_ _ _ _

_ _ _ _

6 The word sunshine is made up of two smaller words (sun + shine). It is called a **compound word**. Use each compound word below in a sentence.

lipstick _____

windmill _____

bedroom _____

toybox _____

birthday _____

7 Use these clues to write list words.

to go on a journey _____

a house on wheels _____

the light from the sun _____

a home on the river _____

remote inland areas _____
     of Australia

| Did you know? |

A pool is a place where we go to swim. But a pool can also be a small area of still water like a puddle or a lake. It can also mean a collection of money put in by different people. If all the children in a class brought along fifty cents each to buy their teacher a gift, we would say they had a pool of money.

Revision

1 Place these words in the correct balloons.

burn	nurse	ground	toast	farmer	south	toad
mice	bike	never	white	purse	mouse	write
coat	under	church	loaf	cloud	fern	

ur
_____
_____
_____

i–e
_____
_____
_____

er
_____
_____
_____

oa
_____
_____
_____

ou
_____
_____
_____

2 Use the words below to label the scene. Then colour the picture.

oak   ribbon   cloud   paddle   coat   hide   boat   bike
nurse   burn   ground   tree   toad   mice   kite   fern

List words

a–e	ai	–ck	–ear	er
cake	pain	back	ear	over
take	main	pack	dear	under
make	rain	sack	near	never
rake	drain	rack	hear	supper
name	brain	tack	clear	later
game	stain	pick	fear	winter
mate	nail	lick	tear	summer
stake	snail	sick	gear	farmer
spade	pail	tick	shear	Easter
made	grain	kick	spear	fern
shade				letter
shake	**ar**	**ea**	**ee**	better
came	card	clean	weed	thunder
same	yard	mean	feed	water
blame	hard	lean	meet	silver
lame	star	bean	seen	corner
wake	far	cream	weep	spider
bake	bar	dream	peep	teacher
lake	shark	leaf	deep	other
safe	part	bread	keep	river
whale	smart	head	sleep	
sale	start	dead	tree	
stale		tea	sheep	
cage		read	green	
		heat		
		neat		
		wheat		
		please		
		real		
		seal		
		meal		
		heal		

i–e	ing	–nk	–nt	oa
ice	king	bank	tent	coat
mice	ring	sank	went	boat
nice	sing	tank	lent	oak
rice	wing	thank	bent	soak
ripe	swing	spank	ant	oats
wipe	thing	pink	pant	toast
white	sting	sink	chant	coast
write	fling	wink	mint	roast
kite	bring	drink	hint	loaf
bike	string	think	print	toad
side	cling	stink		foam
ride	sling	blink	**o–e**	goal
wide	spring	bunk	nose	foal
hide	wring	sunk	rose	moan
tide	single	trunk	hose	goat
slide	jingle	skunk	pole	coach
time	singlet	junk	hole	croak
shine	ringlet	dunk	note	throat
nine		plank	bone	float
mine	**–ng**	blank	cone	groan
	sang		broke	
	song		smoke	
	rang		alone	
	rung		stone	
	fang		joke	
	gang		poke	
	thong		woke	
	wrong		stroke	
	along		spoke	
	lung		choke	
			rope	
			slope	

continued
over page

List words (continued)

or

sort
fort
sport
torn
corn
born
horn
cork
pork
fork

ou

shout
pouch
trout
south
found
ground
round
about
cloud
mouse

ow

low
bow
slow
show
snow
crow
flow
follow
bowl
own
blown
below
elbow
shown
grow
grown
window
throw
tow
blow

sh–

shed
ship
shot
shut
shop
shin
shy
shell
shock
short

–sh

rash
rush
push
wash
bush
brush
crush
fresh
blush
finish

th–

they
them
these
those
this
thin
thick
think
thank
three

–th

moth
cloth
tooth
teeth
mouth
month
path
bath
with
both

ur

turn
burn
curl
hurt
burst
church
fur
nurse
surf
purse

Maths words

numbers
estimate
shapes
square
measure
subtraction
add
answers
circle
counting

Book Week

book
read
page
story
write
author
illustrate
publish
award
cover

Double consonants

letter
better
butter
cuddle
puddle
middle
paddle
summer
ribbon
rubber
dinner
winner
happy
off
stiff
cliff
puff
sell
shell
spell

Space words

space
sun
moon
star
comet
craft
planet
Earth
rocket
Solar System

Sports words

netball
hockey
swimming
diving
cricket
football
running
basketball
tennis
jumping

Holiday words

caravan
sunshine
travel
houseboat
fishing
aeroplane
swimming
beach
outback
pool

Essential words 1

about
after
all
are
back
our
came
could
friend
from
get
going

Essential words 2

because
very
did
just
wish
like
what
make
have
more
house
other

My words

Aa

Bb

Cc

Dd

Ee

Ff

Gg

Hh

Ii

Jj

Kk

Ll

Mm

_____

_____

_____

_____

_____

Nn

_____

_____

_____

_____

_____

Oo

_____

_____

_____

_____

Pp

_____

_____

_____

_____

Qq

Rr

Ss

Tt

Uu

Vv

Ww

Xx Yy Zz

Progress record sheet

Unit		Date completed	Comments
Unit 1	**ar** words		
Unit 2	**sh–** words		
Unit 3	**–sh** words		
Unit 4	**–ck** words		
Unit 5	**th–** words		
Unit 6	**–nk** words		
Unit 7	Maths words		
Unit 8	**–nt** words		
Unit 9	Essential words 1		
Unit 10	Revision		
Unit 11	**–th** words		
Unit 12	More **–nk** words		
Unit 13	**ee** words		
Unit 14	**ai** words		
Unit 15	**ea** words		
Unit 16	Book Week words		
Unit 17	More **ea** words		
Unit 18	**–ng** words		
Unit 19	Essential words 2		
Unit 20	Revision		
Unit 21	**ing** words		
Unit 22	**–ear** words		
Unit 23	**a–e** words		
Unit 24	More **a–e** words		
Unit 25	**o–e** words		
Unit 26	**or** words		
Unit 27	**ow** words		
Unit 28	**i–e** words		
Unit 29	Sports words		
Unit 30	Revision		
Unit 31	More **i–e** words		
Unit 32	**oa** words		
Unit 33	**ur** words		
Unit 34	**er** words		
Unit 35	Double consonants		
Unit 36	More double consonants		
Unit 37	**ou** words		
Unit 38	Space words		
Unit 39	Holiday words		
Unit 40	Revision		

92